Fact Finders®

NASTY (BUT USEFUL!) SCIENCE

ONION JUICE, POOP,
and Other Surprising Sources of
ALTERNATIVE ENERGY

by Mark Weakland

Consultant:
Kevin W. Harrison, PhD
Senior Engineer
National Renewable Energy Laboratory
Golden, Colorado

CAPSTONE PRESS
a capstone imprint

Fact Finders are published by Capstone Press,
1710 Roe Crest Drive, North Mankato, Minnesota 56003.
www.capstonepub.com

 Books published by Capstone Press are manufactured with paper
containing at least 10 percent post-consumer waste.

Library of Congress Cataloging-in-Publication Data
Weakland, Mark.
    Onion juice, poop, and other surprising sources of alternative energy/by Mark Weakland.
    p. cm.—(Fact finders. Nasty (but useful!) science)
    Summary: "Describes the science behind unusual sources of energy that could be used in
place of fossil fuels"—Provided by publisher.
    Includes bibliographical references and index.
    ISBN 978-1-4296-4536-2 (library binding)
    ISBN 978-1-4296-6347-2 (pbk)
    1. Renewable energy sources—Miscellanea—Juvenile literature. 2. Biomass energy—Miscellanea—
Juvenile literature. I. Title. II. Series.
TJ808.2.W43 2011
621.042—dc22   2009050347

Editorial Credits
Jennifer Besel, editor; Matt Bruning, designer; Eric Manske, production specialist

Photo Credits
Alamy: Jim West (farm), 7, Nigel Cattlin (piglets), 11; Capstone Studio: 15, Karon Dubke (fat), 19, Karon
Dubke, 27; Courtesy of Gills Onions, LLC, 17 (both); Courtesy of Katie Fehrenbacher, Earth2Tech, 26;
iStockphoto: Cindy Singleton, 9, Skip ODonnell, 12; Newscom, 21; Shutterstock: Andrey Sukhachev
(bacteria), 25, E.G.Pors (cow), cover, Gilian McGregor (cow), 5, GrigoryL (oil), 19, hilmi (soil), 17, James
Steidl (factory), 5, Kris Butler (algae), 29, Laurence Gough, 23, Maksim Toome (car), 5, Mana Photo
(ocean), 29, Michael Pettigrew (termites), 25, Vasilyev (molecule), 11, Worldpics (sheep), 29, YASAR
(Earth), 5, 29; U.S. Department of Health and Human Services CDC/Don Stalons (bacteria), 7; Visuals
Unlimited/Dennis Kunkel Microscopy (bacteria), 11

Artistic Effects
iStockphoto: Dusko Jovic, javarman3; Shutterstock:belle23, cajoer, Hal_P, krupinina, Pokaz,
Ultrashock, xiver

Printed in the United States of America in North Mankato, Minnesota.
112012
006982R

TABLE OF CONTENTS

CREATIVE ENERGY

Coal, poop, and chicken fat all have something in common. What is it? They're all sources of energy.

Machines that do work, like toasters or bulldozers, are powered by energy. Right now, most of that energy is created by burning **fossil fuels**. But burning these fuels also produces carbon dioxide. This gas causes changes in Earth's climate.

Methane is another climate-changing gas. Methane comes from many sources, including animal farts and poop. Methane and carbon dioxide build up in Earth's atmosphere. The gases keep heat from escaping into space. So Earth gets hotter.

Global warming causes problems for all living things. It leads to droughts in some areas and too much rain in others. Habitats disappear, leaving animals without food or protection. Too much rain floods cities, damaging homes and roads.

fossil fuels: natural fuels like coal or oil

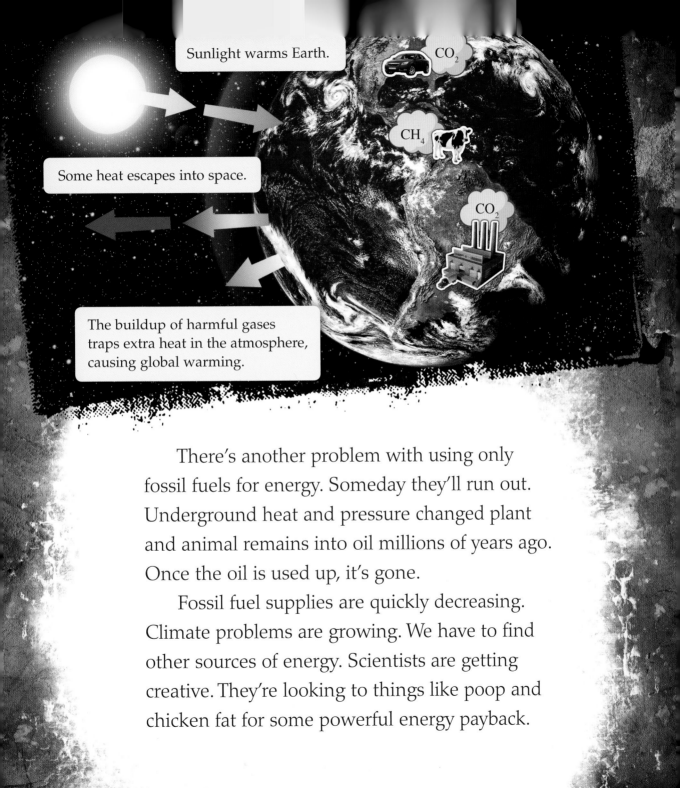

Sunlight warms Earth.

CO$_2$

CH$_4$

CO$_2$

Some heat escapes into space.

The buildup of harmful gases traps extra heat in the atmosphere, causing global warming.

There's another problem with using only fossil fuels for energy. Someday they'll run out. Underground heat and pressure changed plant and animal remains into oil millions of years ago. Once the oil is used up, it's gone.

Fossil fuel supplies are quickly decreasing. Climate problems are growing. We have to find other sources of energy. Scientists are getting creative. They're looking to things like poop and chicken fat for some powerful energy payback.

GOT GAS?

Cows spend most of their day eating and pooping. About 100 million cows live in the United States alone. All that poop piles up. Fortunately, cow poop contains usable energy.

Rising from piles of steaming cow manure is methane gas. Normally methane just floats into the atmosphere, adding to global warming. But if captured, methane can be burned to produce energy. That's right—poop power! Here's how it works.

First, manure is piped into a giant airtight tank called a digester. Then the tank is heated to 100 degrees Fahrenheit (38 degrees Celsius). Tiny organisms called anaerobic bacteria live in the cow poop. These little buggers don't need oxygen. The warm, airless tanks provide a perfect environment for the bacteria to live and reproduce. Inside, bacteria **digest** the plant material in the cow poop. That's why the tanks are called digesters.

digest: to break down food inside the body

2 Then the manure is pumped into the digester tank.

1 Poop, with its bacteria, is pumped from the barn into manure tanks.

anaerobic bacteria

7

As bacteria digest the plant matter, they give off methane and other gases as waste. This process happens in barnyard manure piles too. But in warm, airless tanks, anaerobic bacteria multiply by the billions. And they digest the manure more quickly. In the digesters, lots and lots of methane gas is given off.

Once captured, methane is used to produce energy. Farmers burn this **biogas** to heat their barns and warm the digester tanks. Biogas is also burned by engines to make electricity. The electricity then powers lights, pumps, and other farm equipment. In the future, digestion of cow manure could provide ongoing electricity for 9 million homes. That's a lot of poop power!

Farm animals in the United States produce about 1 billion tons (907 million metric tons) of manure each year.

biogas: the mixture of methane and other gases given off by bacteria that is used as fuel

GASSY GRAZERS

Grazing animals like cows and sheep also burp and fart a lot. These burps and farts are full of gases, including methane. Why are their burps full of gas? Cows and sheep have four stomachs. These stomachs are filled with bacteria that help digestion. As the bacteria digest plant matter, they make methane. Just like in those digester tanks! The animals get rid of the methane in their stomachs by burping and farting. From whatever end it blows, it's a lot of gas. Worldwide, sheep and cows produce about 88 million tons (80 million metric tons) of methane a year.

GAS HOGS

Methane gas drifts off pig poop just like cow manure. U.S. pigs produce almost 110 million tons (100 million metric tons) of poop a year. All that manure produces a lot of methane. Energy experts are turning that gas into **biodiesel** fuel to power cars and trucks. Here's how.

First, poop-filled pigpens are flushed with recycled water. The watery slop is then collected in tanks. As the liquid manure sits, gravity pulls heavier particles of poop toward the bottom. The watery liquid is sucked off the top and reused for flushing the pens. The thicker liquid at the bottom now looks like brown, stinky pancake batter. This "batter" is piped into airtight tanks.

In the warm, airless tanks, bacteria digest the manure. Methane bubbles to the top. A tank covering catches the gas. After the gas is collected, heat and pressure change it into methanol. This fuel is one of the main ingredients in biodiesel.

biodiesel: a liquid fuel made by processing vegetable oils and other fats

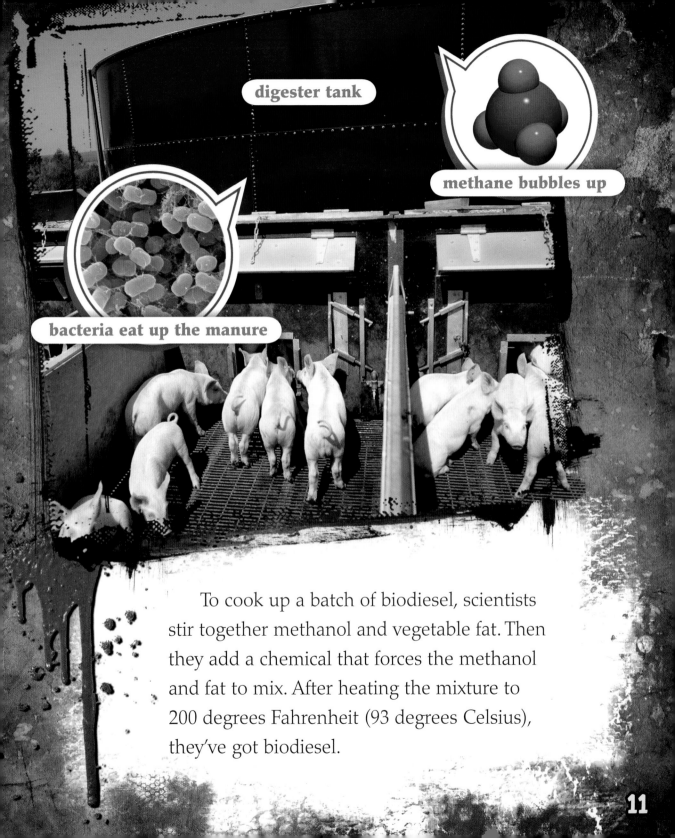

digester tank

methane bubbles up

bacteria eat up the manure

To cook up a batch of biodiesel, scientists stir together methanol and vegetable fat. Then they add a chemical that forces the methanol and fat to mix. After heating the mixture to 200 degrees Fahrenheit (93 degrees Celsius), they've got biodiesel.

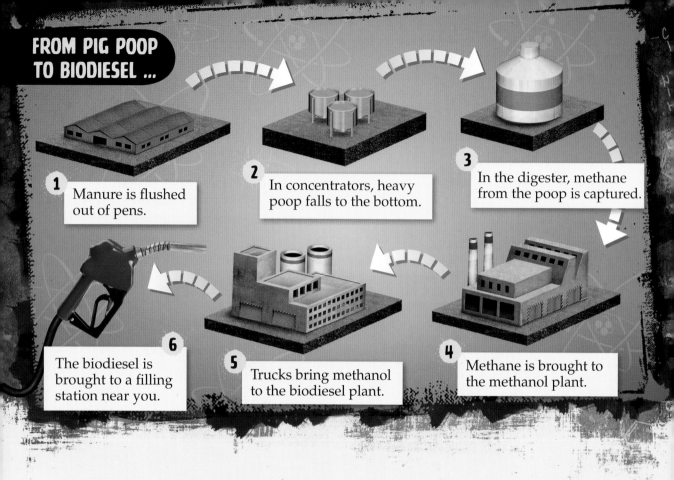

FROM PIG POOP TO BIODIESEL ...

1 Manure is flushed out of pens.

2 In concentrators, heavy poop falls to the bottom.

3 In the digester, methane from the poop is captured.

4 Methane is brought to the methanol plant.

5 Trucks bring methanol to the biodiesel plant.

6 The biodiesel is brought to a filling station near you.

SWEET SMELL OF SUCCESS

Will all of these alternative fuels stink up your life? Don't worry. Fuels made from manure won't make your home smell like a barnyard.

When first collected, manure is stinky. Pig poop is downright foul, and people poop is no bed of roses. But when human and animal waste is stored in tanks or covered lagoons, odors are greatly reduced. And once manure is turned into electricity or biodiesel, the stink is totally gone. Electricity is odorless. And some say biodiesel smells like French fries!

Pig poop stinks but not when it comes to energy. Biodiesel from pig poop burns clean. It doesn't send harmful gases into the air. Biodiesel also provides an alternative to diesel made from fossil fuels. Biodiesel can be used by itself in adapted truck engines. Or it can be mixed with petroleum diesel and burned in a regular engine.

Diesel from pigs is not yet ready for the family car. Right now, pig poop biodiesel contains too much water. But scientists are working to perfect the fuel. When they do, the term "gas hog" will have a whole new meaning.

FOUL FACT

The smell of an animal's poop depends on the food it eats. Meat-eating animals have stinky poop. Rabbits, guinea pigs, and other small plant-eating mammals have sweeter smelling poop. Find some and smell for yourself!

TOILET POWER

Just like cows and pigs, people poop. Now communities around the world are beginning to use people poop to make energy.

Bathroom waste normally flows from toilets to sewers. Sewage treatment plants then store the swirling streams of waste in tanks or lagoons. In the tanks, bacteria digest the solid waste, producing methane gas.

Most sewage plants don't use the gas. They simply vent it into the air, adding to global warming. But in the city of Vancouver, British Columbia, Canada, a treatment plant is capturing the methane. The gas is transported through pipelines into people's homes. It can be burned, just like natural gas, to heat a house or make hot water.

FOUL FACT

On average, a person produces about .5 pound (227 grams) of poop every day.

In India, a company has invented a gas-capturing machine for home use. People place cow manure, kitchen scraps, and human poop into the digester. Bacteria in the cow poop break down the waste and produce methane. The methane flows though a tube into a big plastic storage container. Presto! You've got stored biogas. A family can then use the gas to cook its meals. When the gas runs out, they just add more waste.

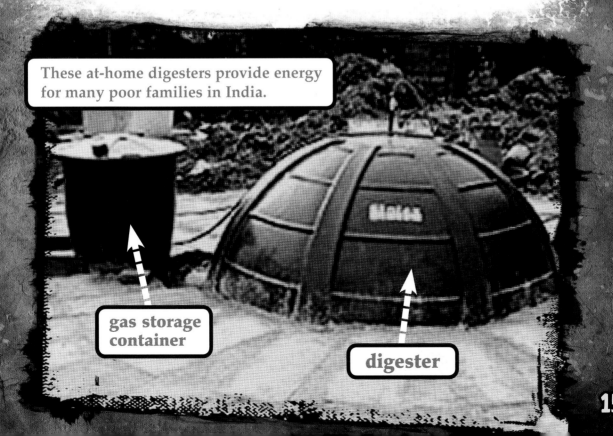

These at-home digesters provide energy for many poor families in India.

gas storage container

digester

ROTTING ENERGY

Poop isn't the only stinky stuff that can be used to make energy. Rotting food is also a source. One energy facility uses rotten tomatoes, spoiled milk, and other kitchen castoffs. The smelly, rotting food is mixed and chopped in a powerful blender. Hot water is added to make a watery stew called slurry.

Cow poop, rich in anaerobic bacteria, is then mixed into the slurry. In the hot sludge, bacteria quickly multiply. They digest **cellulose** present in the vegetable matter. And what do the bacteria produce as they digest the cellulose? Methane! The biogas is stored and then pushed through a pipeline. Once in the pipeline, it's used to power gas lights or to cook food.

cellulose: the substance from which the cell walls of plants are made

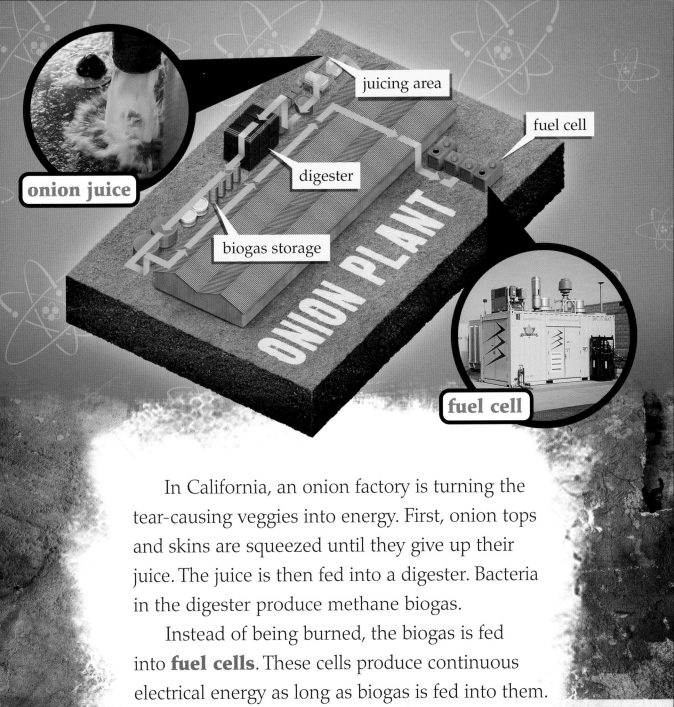

onion juice

juicing area

fuel cell

digester

biogas storage

ONION PLANT

fuel cell

In California, an onion factory is turning the tear-causing veggies into energy. First, onion tops and skins are squeezed until they give up their juice. The juice is then fed into a digester. Bacteria in the digester produce methane biogas.

Instead of being burned, the biogas is fed into **fuel cells**. These cells produce continuous electrical energy as long as biogas is fed into them.

fuel cell: a device that produces electricity by combining a fuel with oxygen

RUNNING ON FAT

Manure isn't the only animal product being used as an energy source. Scientists are trying to cook up batches of biodiesel from animal fats. If they succeed, jiggling lumps of chicken fat may soon power your car.

When scientists make biodiesel, they usually use pig poop and vegetable oil. Vegetable oils are made from corn and soybeans. These oils are expensive. Now scientists are turning to animal fats. The **molecules** of animal fats and vegetable oils are similar in structure.

With the right chemical process, fat molecules can be turned into molecules that are like those of petroleum fuels. In one process, scientists mix chicken fat and **tall oil**. Then they add in methanol. Under heat and pressure, the fat and oil dissolve and react with the methanol. As that happens, biodiesel fuel is created.

molecule: the smallest part of an element that can exist and still keep the characteristics of the element

tall oil: a liquid made from pine trees

vegetable oil molecule

chicken fat molecule

 Oxygen   Carbon   Hydrogen

 **FOUL FACT**

It is possible to make biodiesel fuel from human fat. But it's against the law to do so.

OOZING OIL

Call it poop or call it waste. Whatever its name, it could be worth billions. It's crude oil from microbes, and it might be coming to a gas station near you.

Microbes are single-celled organisms. They are so small you need a microscope to see them. Microbes grow in all types of environments, including your intestines. One such microbe is the bacteria called E. coli.

Like all organisms, E. coli must eat to live. E. coli dine on vegetable matter, like corn and sugarcane. As they eat, they break down vegetable matter into sugars. The bacteria give off molecules of fatty acids as they digest the sugars. Fatty acids are made up of hydrogen, carbon, and oxygen. And as it turns out, these fatty acids are very similar to the molecules of crude oil.

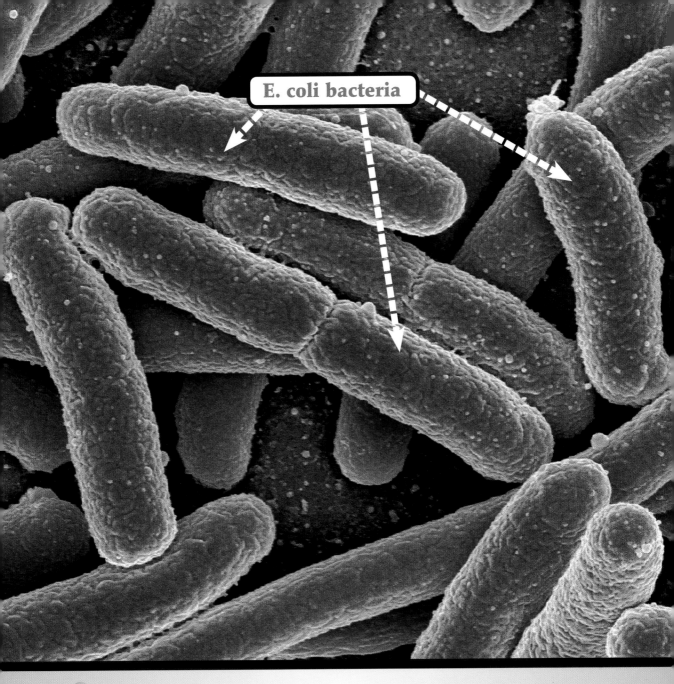

E. coli bacteria

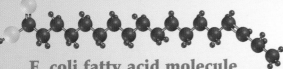

E. coli fatty acid molecule

biofuel molecule

Scientists wondered if they could make E. coli give off biofuel instead of fatty acids. It turns out they could! Scientists changed the bacteria's **DNA**. Now these microbes give off substances that can be burned as car, truck, or even jet fuel.

Fuels made by bacteria have many benefits. The fuels they produce are renewable. As long as the bacteria live and grow, the fuels will flow. And extra carbon dioxide isn't produced. This means the process doesn't contribute to global warming. Bacteria don't need to feed on expensive foods, either. They can eat plant waste like straw, corn stalks, and wood chips.

DNA: the molecule that carries all of the instructions to make a living thing

A BIT AT A TIME

Oil made by bacteria still has problems. For starters, the microscopic creatures produce very small amounts of oil. Only a few hundred gallons can be made at a time. Americans, however, use more than 140 million barrels of oil a week!

Cost and time are other problems. Making the oil takes weeks. And it costs thousands of dollars to make even small amounts of oil. Scientists are hopeful, though. They already have a practice facility open in San Francisco, California. A facility large enough to produce thousands of gallons of this biofuel may be open by 2011.

GRASSOLINE

Today many people use ethanol to power their cars. Ethanol is a fuel currently made from corn. But corn is a food source and it's expensive to grow. Plants like sorghum and switchgrass are cheap and easy to grow. Scientists are trying to find ways to make "grassoline" from these plants. How are they doing it? By studying termites!

It's true that termites are house-eating creepy crawlies. But they're naturals at turning plant matter into energy. Termites could hold the secret to cheap biofuel production.

Termites feast on wood, even though it has almost no nutritional value. The secret to their success is bacteria living in their little bug bellies.

termite's digestive enzymes

First, a termite chomps on wood. The wood contains cellulose. The bacteria in a termite's tummy easily break apart cellulose. They do this by giving off enzymes. These substances break long molecules into short ones. In termite guts, enzymes break long cellulose molecules into short sugar molecules. The sugars are then turned into the energy termites need to stay alive. How sweet it is!

Scientists are studying termites to understand the enzymes that break apart cellulose. They want to reproduce those enzymes in the lab. If scientists can make the enzymes, they'll be able break plant matter into sugars just like the termites. And if they can break down the plants, they'll be able to make ethanol from grasses and trees!

Scientists use huge labs filled with equipment to study tiny termite enzymes.

GUT GOO

Studying enzymes in a termite's gut is tricky business. A scientist holds a frozen termite with a set of needle-nosed tweezers. The termite is then yanked in half. Then its string-like gut is teased out. A tiny swollen bulb sticks out from the end of the gut. Stabbed with a sharp needle, the gut is punctured. It leaks a drop of glistening goo. Jackpot! Inside the goo are the enzymes the scientist needs to study. When the goo is spread on a glass slide, it can be studied under a microscope.

FULL OF ENERGY

Energy sources like poop and fat are stinky and squishy. But they're important. The energy needed to toast our bread has to come from somewhere. If we want electricity for the future, we need alternative energy sources now. Fuels made from gross substances can replace fossil fuels that produce carbon dioxide. In turn, we can slow down global climate change.

Businesses are gearing up to make energy from new sources. Chicken fat and kitchen scraps are being turned into fuels right now. Farmers use biogas from manure to run farm machines. If you haven't been touched by an alternate energy source yet, you will be in the near future. In five to 15 years, millions of gallons of biodiesel could be made from switchgrass. Oils given off by bacteria could produce millions more.

Scientists are looking at other energy sources too. Ocean waves and hydrogen are two possible sources. Another is algae. These ocean plants create fats using only carbon dioxide and energy from the sun. The fats can then be turned into fuel.

In the future, you might discover an insect or plant that can produce nonpolluting energy. Maybe you'll find a way to turn dirty diapers into jet fuel. Or perhaps you'll invent a way to catch methane in sheep burps. In a world where pig poop powers pickup trucks, anything is possible.

GLOSSARY

atmosphere (AT-muhs-feer)—the mixture of gases that surrounds Earth

biodiesel (BI-oh-de-suhl)—a liquid fuel made by processing vegetable oils and other fats

biogas (BI-oh-gas)—the mixture of methane and other gases given off by bacteria that is used as fuel

cellulose (SEL-yuh-lohss)—the substance from which the cell walls of plants are made

digest (dy-JEST)—to break down food inside the body

DNA (dee-en-AY)—the molecule that carries all of the instructions to make a living thing and keep it working

fossil fuels (FAH-suhl FYOOLZ)—natural fuels formed from the remains of plants and animals; coal, oil, and natural gas are fossil fuels

fuel cell (FYOOL CELL)—a device that produces electricity by combining a fuel with oxygen

molecule (MOL-uh-kyool)—the smallest part of an element that can exist and still keep the characteristics of the element

tall oil (TAWL OIL)—an oily liquid made from pine trees

READ MORE

Biskup, Agnieszka. *Understanding Global Warming with Max Axiom, Super Scientist*. Graphic Science. Mankato, Minn.: Capstone Press, 2008.

Cartlidge, Cherese. *Alternative Energy.* Ripped from the Headlines. Yankton, S.D.: Erickson Press, 2008.

Morgan, Sally. *Alternative Energy Sources*. Science at the Edge. Chicago: Heinemann Library, 2010.

O'Neal, Claire. *How To Use Waste Energy to Heat and Light Your Home*. Tell Your Parents. Hockessin, Del.: Mitchell Lane, 2009.

INTERNET SITES

FactHound offers a safe, fun way to find Internet sites related to this book. All of the sites on FactHound have been researched by our staff.

Here's all you do:

Visit *www.facthound.com*

FactHound will fetch the best sites for you!

INDEX